THE
SACRAMENTS
An Introduction

EDGAR (TED) STUBBERSFIELD

DEDICATION

This book is dedicated to my good friend Eric who taught me more fully about God's grace.

LIST OF TABLES

LIST OF ABBREVIATIONS

Ap. Conf	Apology to the Augsburg Confession
LC	Large Catechism of Luther
SC	Small Catechism of Luther
West. Conf.	Westminster Confession
AC	Augsburg Confession
39	39 Articles of the Church of England
HC	The Heidelberg Catechism
SA	Salvation Army, International Headquarters

CONTENTS

INTRODUCTION

In its doctrinal position, my denomination, recognizes two sacraments but says nothing about their nature. This leaves considerable flexibility of belief but the normal position is to see them as empty signs. The sad reality, as shown by the 1996 National Church Life Survey is that they mean little to most members.

As a consequence, I recognize that my training in the sacraments could have been fuller and richer. My denominational lectures did not reveal the depth and strength of the arguments of those holding contrary views. While I have had a strong grounding in the Word, my strengths should be in both word and sacrament. This small work started as an essay for a college in Melbourne and was intended to allow the author to round his education. I needed to address misgivings about the position held by many in my denomination and to come to a richer understanding of the nature and purpose of the sacraments if such a position exists. It was hoped that this study would result in an improved attitude towards and ability to administer the sacraments.

The essay was later expanded into this introduction to the sacraments for Philippine pastors who minister faithfully in remote villages under difficult circumstances. It is hoped that in a small way this effort will build up even in a small way the body of Christ in a part of the world far from my own.

The words in bold type may not be familiar to some readers and their meaning can be found in the Glossary at the end of the essay.

Ted Stubbersfield,
December 1997.

1 THE NUMBER OF SACRAMENTS

The word "sacrament" is derived from the Latin *sacramentum*, and, as such, is not a biblical term. Sacramentum was the word used in the Vulgate to translate the Greek *mysterion (*mystery*)* as found in Eph. 5:32. There it is not an accurate translation as the Greek word is used in a technical sense to describe something that was once hidden but is now revealed, not something that was mysterious. Prior to Christianity, the Latin term meant putting aside as sacred and was a legal term applied to a deposit made by two litigants and placed in a temple before going to court. It was used to describe the "mysteries" of the **mystery religions** and was later applied to the preliminary oath of a Roman soldier. It eventually became a term for any religious engagement[1] (Thomas

[1]In Pliny's letter to Trajan, the word used in this sense when he wrote "they bound themselves with an oath (sacramentum) not for any crime, but not to commit theft or robbery or adultery" (Stevenson 1970, 14)

[2]This similarity in use was recognized by the early church. Justin Martyr in his *First Apology* (Ch. 66) wrote that "The wicked devils have imitated [the Eucharist] in the mysteries of Mithras commanding the same thing to be done." Tertullian also in his *Prescriptions against Heresies* (Ch. 40) when speaking about Mithras said "The Devil . . . by the mystic rites of his idols, vies even with the essential portions of the sacraments of God."

[3]Tertullian in his work *To the Martyrs* (3.1) wrote "we were called to service in the army of the Living God in the very moment when we gave response to the words of the sacramental oath." Frontinus describes the *sacramentum* as the "oath of allegiance administered to them by the tribunes, but they used to pledge each other not to quit the force by flight, or in consequence of fear, and not to leave the ranks except to seek a weapon, strike a foe, or save a comrade" (*Stratagems*, 4.1.4).

1963, 347). While its eventual looser application would cloud the issue of the number of sacraments, its non-Biblical application does help in our understanding of the term. In the mystery religions, it described the actions of their gods who allowed the participants the opportunity to participate in the suffering of their deities[2], while in its use with the legions it described an initiation in which there was no place for the unworthy (Kittel 1967, 826-7)[3]

Before discussing the number of sacraments it would be helpful to understand what a sacrament is. Unfortunately, even a brief examination of the definitions of a sacrament in *Table 1* shows clearly that among the different theologians there is great disagreement. Rather than provide a definition from one of those below - which would entail making a judgement before the strengths of the different views are assessed - this essay will attempt to develop a definition from an examination of the literature and practice.

THE SACRAMENTS - VARIOUS DEFINITIONS	
Augustine	"The visible sign of an invisible thing" (Calvin Institutes 4:13.1)
Calvin	"An external sign by which the Lord seals on our consciences his promises of good-will towards us, in order to sustain the weakness of our faith and we in turn testify our piety towards him, both before himself and before angels as well as men" (Calvin Institutes, 4:13:1)
Luther	It seems proper that those rites be called sacraments which contain promises with signs attached to them. The remainder, not connected with signs, are only promises (Plass 1972, 1235).
Zwingli	Sacraments are "signs by which a man approves himself to the church as a disciple, or soldier, and the effects of the sacraments is rather to give assurance of faith to the Church than any assurance to the person himself" (Thomas 1963, 360)
Aquinas	The sacramental signs became divinely endowed or invested with a certain quality, and that God gave his grace to the recipients therein and thereby (Thomas 1963, 358).

Table 1

The church in the Middle Ages exercised almost complete control over the lives of its subjects through its many sacraments. Not only were they used to regulate Christian worship but they also controlled birth, marriage and death (Bainton 1969, 46). Christianity, for the most part, was really based on administering the sacraments, as prayers were in Latin and, a largely uneducated clergy was only obligated to preach quarterly (Ryle 1981, 38). It is not surprising that the Reformers would attack at the point of the sacraments, removing their tyranny and restoring the word to the people.

When the term sacrament lost its specific meaning it became broadly associated with any sacred act of the church.[4] The creed was spoken of as "a sacrament" (Thomas 1963, 347), while Augustine (354-430) used the term for all the sacred ceremonies including exorcism, prayer and spiritual songs (1997 De Symbolo ad Catechumenos, 2, 15). Gradually it took on its specific meaning of those special signs. Even during the Middle Ages, however, the word would still be applied to many ceremonies with little discussion as to the precise number of the sacraments. Peter Lombard (1095-1160), one of the earliest systematic theologians of the church, addressed the subject of the number of sacraments and found seven and seven only. His doctrine of the sacraments[5], however, was not as dogmatic though as later Catholicism (Fieser 1996).

To the Roman Catholic, there is now no question as to the number of sacraments. The church spoke authoritatively at the Council of Trent (1547) where it *anathematises* all who say that there are fewer or more than seven (Session VII, Cannon 1). As well as baptism and communion, Trent confirmed Confirmation, Penance, Orders, Matrimony and Extreme Unction as the sacraments. Most protestant churches would say that there are only two - baptism

---

[4]Hugo of St Victor in his treatise *On the Sacraments of the Christian Faith* lists 30 sacraments (Schwarz, 1985, 54).

[5]Found in his fourth book of the *Sentences.*

and communion.

According to Roman Catholic Teaching, the sacraments remind their members of the sacred number seven and correspond to the stages of human growth and the perfecting of society. These are shown in *Table 2* opposite. The Catholic believes that he is flooded with supernatural sacramental grace from birth to death. The Protestant would ignore the harmony of these seven and look only for a Biblical foundation without seeking any support from the church fathers.

ROMAN UNDERSTANDING OF NATURAL AND SPIRITUAL COUNTERPARTS	
Sacrament	Natural Equivalent
Baptism	Birth
Confirmation	Growth
Eucharist	Nourishment
Penance	Healing
Extreme Unction	Death
Orders	Perfecting of society
Marriage	
(Burkouwer 1969, pp 29-30)	

Table 2

Both Rome and the Protestants claim divine institution to support their number of sacraments. At stake is not just a minor matter of categorising but a very different understanding of the nature of grace. *Table 3* contrasts the Catholic and Reformed viewpoint on the seven sacraments

DIFFERENT UNDERSTANDINGS OF SACRAMENTAL GRACE			
Sacrament	**Catholic Authority**	**Classical Catholic viewpoint**	**Reformed viewpoint**
Baptism	Acts 3:37-41	Supernatural grace given in baptism can be lost through mortal sin (Fanning 1996)	No grace is given at baptism as the child is already a Christian (Calvin *Institutes 4 xvi, 20*)
Penance	John 20:22ff	Post baptismal sins can be forgiven through the men whom Christ gave this authority and power (Matros 1981, 322)	Penance devalues baptism cutting the believer off from the baptismal promises and transfers them to another sacrament (Calvin *institute*s 4 xix 8).
Confirmation	John 3	Baptismal grace is strengthened through the laying on of hands and the gift of the Holy Spirit (Matros 1981, 211).	It abolishes the intention and power of baptism replacing it with an ordinance that promises more. (Calvin *Institutes* 4 xix 10&11).
Extreme Unction	James 5:14	A completion of baptism and penance, to give help and strength before	The days of miracles are past and forgiveness of sins comes by confession not by a power

		a person enters the presence of his Judge or to heal the sick (Matros 1981, 381).	inherent in a sacrament. (Calvin, *Institutes* 4 xix 18&21).
Holy Orders	Exodus 28-29	Supernatural grace is given whereby a visible priest is endued with power to consecrate and forgive (Matros 1981, 471).	Priesthood is a gift to the whole church and the faithful must not be robbed of what is theirs (Calvin *Institutes* 4 xix 25).
Marriage	Ephesians 5:28, 32	Confers a new similarity to Christ who is married to the church. It brings an increase in grace (Matros 1981, 406).	Marriage is a holy ordinance but similarities to divine examples do not make sacraments otherwise there would be no end to them (Calvin *institutes* 4 xix 34).
Eucharist	Matthew 26:26-29	The mass is a sacrifice offered up to God by man. The elements become the actual body and blood of Christ (Phole 1996).	Christ offered himself in sacrifice sanctifying us forever and purchasing eternal redemption (Calvin *institutes* 4 xviii 3).

Table 3

Berkouwer (1969 40) summarizes the fundamental difference between Rome and the reformers over the number of sacraments:

> "Because the sacraments are interpreted as ever renewed infusions of grace, they acquire their character as mystery. The Reformation in contrast emphasises the involvement of the sacrament with the mystery"

The Protestant Church maintained that if there were not strict rules by which to judge a sacrament then it would be impossible to limit the number to even the seven of Catholicism. Some of the criteria given are listed in *Table 4* below.

PROTESTANT CRITERIA FOR A SACRAMENT		
LUTHERAN (Ap. Conf VII, 3)	**ANGLICAN** (Thomas, 1963, 353)	**CALVIN** (*Institutes* 4. XIX, 1)
1. Rites commanded by Christ	1. Appointed by Christ	1. "Consecrated with (Christ's) own lips"
2. To which is added the promise of grace	2. An outward sign	2. "Distinguished by excellent promises"
	3. An inward grace	

Table 4

Generally the reformers decided on the two sacraments, baptism and eucharist though in the very early days there was some indecision. Luther in his *larger catechism* (1529) retained two but in the *Apology to the Augsburg Confession* (VII, 4) Absolution was included - a view originally accepted by the Anglicans under Cranmer (Thomas, 1963. 352). This third sacrament dropped away[6] as it became understood that Lutheran absolution differed from Catholic penance. Melanchthon argued for the inclusion of ordination (Schmidt, 1961, 525) but this did not gain any acceptance from the Lutherans. As the work of the reformation became established it settled firmly on the two sacraments only[7].

SACRAMENTAL PROMISES	
Communion	Baptism
A new covenant Matt 26:28, Union with Christ in God's kingdom Matt 26:29, Salvation of many Mk 14:24, Union with each other 1 Cor 17-22, Christ's loving discipline I Cor 11:27-32	Christ's continuing presence Matt 28:29, Personal salvation. Mk 16:16, An overcoming faith Mk 16:17-18, The baptism in the Holy Spirit Acts 1:5, Forgiveness of sins Acts Acts 2:38. A family salvation Acts 2:39

Table 5.

---

[6]The Anglican church only adopted the two sacrament view in its 38 articles of 1563.

[7]Though not generally accepted within Lutheranism it would appear that on the basis of the Ap. Conf. that a Lutheran is free to accept absolution as a sacrament (Schmidt, 1963, 525). While their freedom from human commands allows this, confession is generally seen as a stumbling block. as an intermediary introduced to the sacraments is unnecessary as it should be totally God's work. (Liebeldt, Pers. Comm. 1997).

In their rejection of the additional five Catholic sacraments[8], the Reformed and Lutheran churches drew a clear distinction between sacraments and ceremonies of the church (eg Calvin, *Institutes,* 4 XIX 2), for not to do so would increase the sacraments well beyond even the seven of Rome. They rejected also any argument from the later traditions of the church. They did, however, find support for their two sacrament stance in the belief of the early church. As already shown from Augustine, the church could be very loose in its use of the word *sacrament,* but it was also understood in a very definite sense for baptism and eucharist[9]. Augustine wrote:

> "Our Lord Jesus Christ (as he himself says in his gospel) has placed us under a yoke which is easy, and a burden which is light. Hence he has knit together the society of his new people by sacraments, very few in number, most easy of observance and most excellent in meaning; such is baptism consecrated by the name of the trinity: such is the communion of the body and blood of the lord and any other if recommended in the canonical Scriptures" (Institutes 4 XIX 3)

---

[8]These are sometimes referred to as the sacraments of the church.
[9]These are sometimes referred to as the sacraments of the gospel.

Similarly, Chrysostom speaking of the blood and water that came from Christ's side, stated "...the church exists by these two, and those who are introduced into the full knowledge of our faith know that while they are regenerated by water they are nourished by the body and the blood (Thomas 1963, 348)

Bishop Andrewes puts the Protestant position clearly when he says:

> "For more than a thousand years the number of seven sacraments was never heard of. How then can the belief in seven sacraments be catholic, which means, always believed" (Thomas, 1963, 354)

A Protestant does not have the benefit of a church that can speak authoritatively, and must look firstly at the bounds placed on him/her by a belief of scripture only, and secondly at his/her understanding of grace derived from them. He/she can only decide for two sacraments and finds that the practice of the early church supports his position. For the Protestant, those signs that he calls sacraments will be the ones that were instituted by Christ and, through his word, have a promise attached to them. It would not be unscriptural to see a third, Confession, but in the sense of an implied sacrament. This is because access to the Lords Supper is through a believer examining his own heart, 1 Cor 11. Forgiveness and absolution for a protestant must be rooted in the authority of the word of God which reveals a gracious and forgiving God, not in the priestly office of the minister.

2 SACRAMENTAL FOUNDATIONS

In the Old Testament signs preceded the actions of God. These took many forms, they could be dreams and visions, Isa 6; Jer 1:11-13, unique occurrences, Isa 38:8, prophetic fulfilment, Isa 36:10, even sacramental rites and miracles. These were all intended to show God's power over his creation and his saving work in history. The Christian sacraments did not happen in a vacuum without any signs pointing towards them. They can no more be separated from the history of Jesus Christ than they can be separated from its Old Testament antecedents. Jesus Christ cannot be accepted as Lord outside of an acknowledgement of the fulfilment of the Old Testament promises and the end of the Law (Schlink 1969, 11). Schlink states:

> "The specifics of Christian Baptism can be recognized only as one takes note of the connection and the differences between Christian Baptism and John's Baptism and, beyond that, between Christian Baptism and Old Testament and Jewish ablutions. In the same way the Lord's supper must be understood not only on the basis of Jesus' last meal with his disciples and also his previous table fellowship with sinners and his promise of the

coming meal in the Kingdom of God – as well the Old Testament about covenant meal and sacrifice." (Schlink 1969, 12)

The Foundation of Baptism

The Old Testament has many examples of ritual cleansing by sprinkling or washing, (Lev. 11-15, cf 6:20ff, 16:24ff, 17:15ff and Num. 19.). These covered a wide range of defilement and through these washings the defiled were re-admitted into fellowship. Many prophetic utterances referred to them (Isa. 1:15-16, Jer. 4:14) but not to the outward ritual of washing but the repentance associated with them, Isa. 1:16-17. These washings took on more signifigance during the inter-testamental period, possibly because of the prophesies of Ezekiel 17:1-12 with the flood coming from the sanctuary and Zechariah 13:1 of the fountain in Jerusalem. The cleansing of the whole body became more important and baths, called *miqveh*, were built at many homes as well as synagogues and the temple. Full immersion was required before entry to the temple (Adamthwaite 1992, 42). The Jewish *Mishnah* contains ten chapters about the ritual immersion pool.[10] Baptismal movements grew up in Palestine, the most important being the Essenes, and while not being in this group, ritual washings were very important for the Pharisees. The important feature of this "baptism" is that it was repeated often.

---

[10] Between 1970-80, 48 of these pools were discovered and they all conformed to the Mishnah's requirements of a minimum of 300 litres (40 seahs) and a water depth of 47 inches and with stairs going in and out to stop the purified touching the un-baptised. The seas and flowing rivers could also be used)

The practice called *proselyte baptism* is believed to have developed before John the Baptist, This was the process by which a gentile became accepted as a Jew. It required circumcision, baptism and a blood offering. Confession of sin was not a part of this conversion. After the ceremonies the Gentile was said to have been born again (Edersheim 1977, Appendix XII). They had a new legal status. This baptism differed from the ritual washings in that it was not repeated.

Into this context of baths and washings and baptisms John the Baptist proclaimed his message of repentance, reviving the prophetic message of the day of the Lord's wrath, Matt. 3:9-10. John was aware that he was a forerunner of the coming Messiah, Mk. 1:7. Because God's judgement was imminent, the need for repentance was urgent. This was not some often repeated, self administered external ritual but required confession and turning away from sin, Matt. 3:8. It was a "...preparing of the whole man for his encounter with the coming Judge (Sasse 1977, 18) This was more than a public confession of sin but an empowerment to live a holy life as the fruits of repentance and safety in judgement were expected to follow. Matthew described it, not a baptism *of*, but *for* repentance.   While Jesus forgave sins himself, which is the core of the gospel, John with his baptism did not. It was no more than a preparation to meet the one who baptises in the Holy Spirit and fire.

There are similarities between the baptisms of John and Jesus, John's baptism was dissimilar to what went before. Had it been similar he would not have attracted the title of *the Baptist* nor his baptism been so controversial. John summonsed the whole nation, not just the spiritual elite as did the Essenes. His baptism would have been an insult to the Jews because he lowered them to the same level as the Gentiles. Jesus acknowledged John's special message. Sasse states of Jesus' submission to John's baptism that "...Through the decent of the Spirit upon Christ, John's Baptism became Christian Baptism in its most proper sense. For this reason it has been said again and again in the course of church history that Christian Baptism rests on the Baptism of John." (1969, 21). This submission to a baptism of repentance by the sinless Son is normally regarded as Jesus aligning himself with the sinners he came to redeem, Matt. 3:15, John 1:29.

The Foundation of the Lord's Supper

According to the accounts in the Synoptic Gospels, Jesus instituted the sacrament of communion during a Passover meal. In John's Gospel we read that Jesus was crucified on the afternoon before the Passover cf John 18:28, 19:14, 31. Whether this was a *kiddush*, a preparatory meal, (Bromilley 1987, Vol 3, 165) or the Passover itself with the second holy day in the Paschal week ahead (Edersheim 1977, 613) is not important. The whole meal is charged with the atmosphere and imagery of the Passover and as such it was a remembrance of the time when the mighty hand of God was shown. In this setting Jesus said "do this in remembrance of me" as his own death would be an exodus, Lk. 9:30, which worked a much greater salvation.

In the exodus, the Jews knew that God had shown his power and majesty in history, but this intervention was not just for the generation enslaved in Egypt but was regarded as God's once and for all deliverance involving not only that generation but all that succeed it. Not only did it bring back thankful memories but brought all generations under its eschatological power. In the same manner Jesus was saying the power and reality of his death will bear upon each generation (Bromilley 1987, Vol 3, 165). The Passover, with the killing of the Passover lamb, sprinkling of its blood and eating its flesh brought protection from God's anger and his favour. When Jesus substituted his own broken body and shed blood, he spoke of the same protection and favour being extended to his disciples.

The words that Jesus used at the supper were chosen to give the meal a covenantal nature. When God made his covenant with Israel in Sinai it was followed by a meal in which people, ate drank and saw God (Ex. 24:11). The meal ratified the agreement between the Lord and his people. The idea of a covenant meal goes to the very beginning of Israel's history (Gen 26:30, 31:54, 2 Sam 3:20).

In the Passover the Jews looked to the future deliverance which the Exodus foreshadowed. A cup was set aside for the Messiah, and it may have been this cup that Jesus took to institute the New Covenant. For the Jew, the Passover was a foretaste of the Messianic banquet and a sign of the presence of God in their midst.

3 THE NATURE OF SACRAMENTAL GRACE

Non Sacramental Christianity

While church attendance is low the number of Australians professing to be Christian is very high[11] it would appear the sacraments have little relevance to most "Christians". We need not look any further than the nominalism of faith for an answer to current attitudes to the sacraments. Surprisingly a sacrament free Christianity has arisen among believers who were anything but nominal - the most notable of these being the Society of Friends (Quakers) and the Salvation Army

The Salvation Army is rich in symbolism seen by its use of a flag, uniform, crest and their holiness table. it is surprising, therefore, that it has rejected the symbolism of the sacraments. Untill 1883 the Army was a sacramental church practising both infant baptism and communion. William and Catherine Booth, the founding father and mother of the Army, came to the position of rejecting these rites but from two different viewpoints. General Booth's concern was that every aspect of Army life should help, not hinder their "great end". He saw its potential for divisiveness as being greater that the blessings received (Booth 1996). Catherine,

---

[11]The percentage claiming to be Christian in the 1991 Australian Census for my own electorate is 84%.

however, was driven by the need to see signs of true holiness and was "...horrified of anything that might tend to substitute in the minds of the people some outward act of compliance for the fruits of practical holiness" (Booth 1996)[12]   Catherine was impressed by the genuineness of the Quakers and gave the Army its theology of life itself being a lifelong sacrament (Booth 1996).   This was a theology very similar to that of the Quakers

The Army pointed to what it sees as the inherent dangers in the sacraments. This are listed below:

> 1. Those who are"...destitute of spiritual communion with him" trusting in their ability to receive grace through a ritual" which has its own power (S.A. 1969, 188, 182);

> 2. Trusting that by participating in the rite people were guaranteed of receiving the inward grace it signifies (S.A. 1969, 182);

> 3. The trouble that disputes about the sacraments have wrought in the church, much of this being over trivial matters of form (S.A. 1969, 183); and.

> 4. The appointment of ordained men to be the only channel through which grace can be dispensed (S.A. 1969, 183).

While not having sacraments as such, a Salvationist retains a strong concern "...over the spiritual realities these practices symbolize" (S.A. 1969, 180). It does this by reducing the sacraments to their spiritual core. For communion, it is Jesus as

---

[12]This Internet reference is on work on the sacraments by General Bramwell Booth found in Staff Review, Volume 2, Pages 51-60.

the source of eternal life, and for baptism it is the transforming effect of salvation. Both carry the idea of being brought into fellowship with the church (S.A. 1969, 180). All of this is an act of faith and the sacraments only attest to the work already done in the believer. While faith and repentance can be performed by anyone at anytime, sacraments, however, are not so flexible. The sacraments are seen as a means of grace and almost anything can be sacramental. Each meal can be a sacrament while *The Soldiers Covenant*, by which a person becomes a member of the Army, can take the place of baptism. The Salvationist would therefore claim to live a life surrounded by sacraments without ever partaking of communion or baptism.

Burkouwer (1969, 16) correctly commented that "...if the sacrament is only a secondary symbol, an illustration, then according to this view. It could be dispensed with" and the Army has only taken its theology to its logical conclusion. This chapter considers whether there is a reality beyond the symbols and, if grace is to be received from them, what the nature of this grace is.

There is contrasting theology between the reality of Rome and the symbolism of the Reformation (Berkouwer 1963, 57). Yet if we understand the sacraments to be inactive symbols, a *nuda signa*, then it would be misleading to say most of the Reformers did not have a symbolic doctrine. It is better to see the difference as being between reality and belief. *Sola Fide* is the foundation of the Reformation and for them there was a sacramental reality, but it was "...a reality that existed only for belief and through belief" (Berkouwer 1963, 58)[13]. Rome, on the other hand, would say that

---

[13]Lutheran theology would correctly stress that there is a four fold foundation, *Sola Scriptura, Sola Christo, Sola Gratia* as well as *Sola Gratia*. None stands independent of

if salvation was totally through faith there was no place for the sacraments. The Catholic, Bartmann, stated:

> "The Reformers had no place in their system of *sola fide* for an outward efficacious means of grace. The sacrament can at most be an outward guarantee or proclamation of forensic justice" (Berkouwer 1963, 56).

His warning is quite valid and we find today a loss of sacramental interest, or what Tilloch termed the "death of the sacraments" (Braaten 1983, 87). If Bartmann has correctly assessed the Reformers' sacramental position, then the non sacramental Quakers and the Army represent the most courageous and correct protestant expression on the sacraments. It is not enough to observe the sacraments simply because Jesus commanded it, for as a practice it is hollow without a theology of why he commanded it (Baillie U.D., 40)[14].

Roman Catholic View

For the Catholic there is no doubt as to the nature of sacramental grace, for the church has again spoken with authority (at Trent) on this subject by saying:

---

the other.

[14]The writer's own church observes the Lord's supper weekly and was surprised with the results of the 1997 National Church Life Survey which showed that it was a meaningful experience to only approximately 6% of the assembly.

"If anyone shall affirm that by the very sacraments of the new law this grace is not confirmed ***ex opere operato***, but that only belief in the divine promise is sufficient to obtain grace, let him be accursed"

By working *ex opere operato*[15], which means "by virtue of the action", the sacraments are said to "...cause that grace in the soul of man" (Kennedy 1996,.4), as well as having the power to sanctify (Trent Sess. XIII, Cap.3). It is not dependant on the faith of the recipient, provided they do not put obstacles in the way. The New Testament sacraments are not said to signify and promise salvation but to contain and distribute it. The two effects of the working of the sacraments are shown in *Table 6.*

SACRAMENTAL NATURE ACCORDING TO ROME	
Baptism Penance	Sacraments of Death - for those who are dead because of original or actual sin
Mass Orders Marriage Unction Confirmation	Sacraments of Life - giving an increase of sanctifying grace to those already in a state of grace

Table 6   (Kennedy, 1996, 11)

When attempting to prove the Catholic doctrinal position "...it must be born in mind that [their] rule of faith is not simply scripture, but scripture and tradition" (Kennedy 1996, 5) and many

---

[15]The doctrine is termed *opus operatum.*

quotations from the fathers can be given to support their position. This has set them at odds to the Reformers who, through a foundation of scripture only, stressed the inability of the sacraments to impute grace outside of faith, an action they termed *ex opere operantum* (by the work of an agent). Rome would reject any Protestant claim of magic by also emphasising its doctrine of the unity of opposing parts (*Complexio oppositorum*) which stresses both grace and freedom in salvation. So this sacramental grace works objectively yet requires a disposition towards that grace. This seems contradictory to the Protestant but the Catholic experiences these opposites harmoniously.

Protestant View

The Reformers would reject both causation and preparation (faith) as the means by which the sacraments convey blessing. For the Reformers there was no impersonal grace at work in the sacrament. Sacramental grace was nothing other than a "...gracious personal relationship" (Baillie U.D., 49) stemming from salvation in Christ through faith. They also rejected that the sacraments depend on human faith, rather that they work through faith which is a gracious gift of God (Eph. 2:8). They saw the relationship between faith and sacrament as similar to that of faith and justification expressed in the doctrine of *sola fide*, an often misunderstood doctrine. The Reformers were clear to separate faith from any associated merit. Things are not accomplished by faith but by grace through God-given faith. The Reformers saw the sacraments as directed towards this faith which it strengthened

and nourished (West. Conf. XIV.1). This grace was not seen as an individual gift but directed towards the church, connecting the individuals in their common faith (Schlink 1972, 76).

On the basis of the Great Commission, Luther would not separate sacramental grace and discipleship and he was careful to introduce a thorough system of catechisis. Biblical teaching outside of a strong sacramental system was dangerous and could result in works righteousness, Luther referred to the two men on the road to Emmaeus, Luke 24. Though their hearts burned when they were systematically taught by Christ, their eyes were not opened till Christ broke bread with them. Bonhoffer wrote of the role of catechesis in the church saying it "does not want to bring about competence, build character, or produce certain types of persons. Instead it uncovers sin and creates hearers of the gospel" (Wagner, 1997, 109). In this manner people are prepared to receive the grace of the sacraments.

Zwingli - A Dissenting Voice

Huldrych Zwingli (1484-1531) has been called the third man of the reformation. He saw himself as being more thoroughgoing than Luther in his reformation, ridding the Zurich church of everything that he saw as an accretion from Rome (Gabler 1987, 135). Zwingili, on the basis of John 6:36, stressed the separation of the physical and spiritual. He took a radical position totally rejecting the sacraments not only as a means of salvation (Gabler, 1987, 132) but as even giving any grace at all. This stripped the clergy of any power over souls and reduced them to mere instruments in God's service (Rilliet 1964, 113). The sacraments were seen as a pledge, committing whoever received them to live accordingly

(Rilliet 1964, 115). Zwingli claimed that sacraments were pure symbolism demonstrating to the church and the world that the recipient was a Christian "...just as the white cross worn on the garment of a Swiss Confederate made him recognizable as a Swiss Confederate" (Sasse 1985, 40). There was no necessary connection between the timing of the sign and the inner reality (Rilliet 1964, 114).

The words "act of thanksgiving" was the term Zwingli preferred to use instead of sacrament. As a person took the sacrament (an enacted parable) gratitude was aroused in the memory and drew the believers together (Gabler 1987, 134). This was the most a person could hope from the sacraments. Luther saw this teaching as even more dangerous than the errors of the Papists and saw in his opposition to Zwingli a battle against Satanic forces (Gabler 1987, 134). During Zwingli's lifetime, he did not have the same impact as Luther and Calvin, but his influence has increased over the years. Directly traceable to Zwingli are the **Anabaptists** (Estep 1986, 10) Quakers and other smaller groups (Estep 1986, 203-232) who took his symbolic understanding to its logical end (Gabler 1987, 130).

Assessment

In weighing up the different views on the sacraments, it could be concluded that it is important to link them to God's promise, both as portrayal and confirmation. Do they just point to the blessings they represent or are the blessings communicated in some way? While a distinction must be made between the sign and what is signified, they should neither be separated into two independent units nor at the same time fused as in *ex opere operato*. In the representing and acceptance of God's promises, faith is not just encouraged but strengthened. It does this by encouraging the believer to rest in Christ's completed work and his gracious acceptance of them (West. Conf. XIV.2). Faith which trusts in the truthfulness of God refuses to separate the sign from the promises and those who accept the promise through God-given faith are also receiving Christ and his gifts. Sacramental grace can be nothing less than God's self-giving of himself.

4 SACRAMENTS AND THE WORD

The Word's self attestation is that it is not a lifeless instrument that the Spirit uses, Heb. 4:12, nor is it something that the Spirit can connect himself to and operate through as if he is ordinarily separated from it, John 1:1-2. The Word is God's self disclosure of himself and is inseparable from his own being and in the giving of himself he gives his Word Rom 10:8. It does not act externally and, its convincing power is not eloquence Rom 10:17, but is endowed with efficacy, 1 Pet. 1:23. From the moment it is uttered, the Spirit is inseparably and continually connected with it (Schmidt 1961, 105). Just as God created the universe from nothing, Gen 1, by his word which also sustains it, Heb 1:3, so that which is acceptable in the heart of man is also created and sustained. The Words continual application is intended to sanctify the heart, Eph 5:26, and give hope for the future, Col 1:5, however it does not always achieve its intended results, but instead hardens the heart Heb 6:4-6. But what is meant by *the Word*? The Reformed church has a narrow view. It is the Word written and preached (Calvin, *Institutes* 4.3.8), yet Word is difficult to clearly define. Sasse (1989, 83), the Lutheran theologian wrote:

> "One must always keep in mind that the Word - or a
> particular Word - exists in various forms: in the

heart of God, going out of his mouth, coming to his prophet, heard by him, proclaimed by him, written in Scripture, read, learned, remembered, translated, accompanying the dying soul - always the same powerful and living Word.

To this list should be added preaching and the greatest Word, Christ himself, John 1.

There are three principle forms of the audible Word, (that is, heard, read and preached). The promises of God's Word recited at the sacrament are often little understood at the time of baptism and the first communion but they proclaim the sacrament's authority and the promises attached to them. Again and again, this Word of promised faithfulness can be returned to with increasing understanding and faith, reflected upon and can enter the very core of a person's character and faith. The Scriptures give a setting into which the sacrament fits, not as an isolated incident, but part of an integrated proclamation of a man lost in a sin and a God who, through his actions in history, graciously redeems those who could not redeem themselves. In preaching, the gospel is presented and represented and, by faith, the heart affirms and appropriates its truth. The sacraments cannot be considered outside of its relationship to the Word as they also are a self revelation of God and his redemptive Word and so a Word itself - a visible Word. Rejecting the sacraments means a truncated view of the Word as God's self disclosure (Schwarz, 1985, 58).

Prior to the Reformation, the "visible word" was elevated above the "audible word" but Luther placed them on an equal[16] footing

The Reformed church acknowledged the sacraments as important but, because it was the Word that made them a sacrament, they saw them as *secondary* and additional (HC, Q.66), strengthening the work of the Word (HC, Q.65) which in itself was sufficient (Berkouwer, 1969, 49). If they are secondary and do not add to the clarity of the Word it begs the question of whether they are dispensable (Calvin, *Institutes* 4.14.5). Calvin arguement that, just as important documents need a seal, so also the Word needs a seal, seems inadequate. The scripture indicates that the deep sealing of the truth of the gospel is done in a man's heart,[17] 2 Cor 1:22, Eph 1:13, 4:30, and does not suggest its need for constant reinforcement, The spiritual effect is the greatest seal of a work of God, 1 Cor 9:2, rather than the word being sealed by the sacrament. It is the Word which gives sacraments their relevance (Watson 1966, 161)

---

[16]"Through the Word and the sacraments, as through instruments, the Holy Spirit is given, and the Holy Spirit produces faith where and when it pleases God, in those who hear the gospel" (CA5)

[17]For an in-depth examination of this sealing in the heart see Martin Lloyd Jones, *Romans, The Sons of God*, Ch. 16-30.

5 BAPTISM

Baptism, an act of admission into the church, is universally seen as representing :

> 1. The acceptance of the offer of eternal life and consequent purging from sin by forgiveness,
>
> 2. Sanctification by the Holy Spirit through putting to death our flesh through union with Christ's death,
>
> 3. A testimony before men.

Its practice, however, is varied among the branches of the church. Its differences are clearly seen in the ages of those who normally receive this sacrament, (as infants or adults). Some define this difference as infant or believer's baptism. However, this examination will attempt to show such a clear distinction cannot be made

Protestant Adult Baptism

Apart from the mode, sprinkling or immersion, there is no real difference between the churches in the Reformed, Lutheran or

Baptist tradition. The Reformed writer John Murray stated that "...in the case of adults we baptise on the basis of an intelligent and credible confession" (1980, 55). All groups would readily regard this as an acceptable grounds to offer baptism to an adult. It is their dealing with the children of baptised believers that great differences can be seen. We will consider each of these.

Infant Baptism

(a) Roman Baptism

The Roman church has a history of teaching spanning almost 2000 years from which to draw upon when formulating its doctrine of baptism. This includes not only the scriptures, but the fathers, church councils and Papal encyclicals. There are two main authoritative statements: The *Decree for the Armenians,*[18] a positive statement of what baptism is; and the Council of Trent (Session VII, *De Baptismo*) where it is stated what baptism is not. In the former we read:

> "The effect of this sacrament is the remission of all sins, original and actual, likewise of all punishment which is due for sin. As a consequence, no satisfaction for past sin is enjoined upon those who are baptised; and if they die before they commit any sin, they attain immediately to the kingdom of heaven and the vision of God" (Fanning 1996).

---

[18]This is often referred to as the Council of Florence and is found in Papal Bull *Exultae Deo* by Pope Eugene IV

The Council of Trent was a response to the Reformation and many of its "strange and novel theories" (Fanning 1996, 18) on baptism were anathematized. Rome's strong and authoritative stance at Trent has left it in a no compromise position against the views of Calvin, Luther and Zwingli.

Because the sacraments operate *ex opere operato*, and children cannot place an impediment in the way, they receive the full infusion of baptismal grace and gifts. Firstly, original sin is removed, (Ez 36:25, Eph 5:25, Acts 32:16) as well as actual sin (Trent Sess 5, Orig. Sin 5) which will see the child's adoption as sons of Christ and assure the receipt of heavenly grace (Trent, VI, ch 7). Baptism places an indelible stamp upon the soul (Trent V11 Can.ix) and confers the special graces necessary to achieve the end of baptism and the fulfilment of baptismal promises. If a person was to die immediately after baptism "...there will be absolutely nothing that a man must answer for he will have been freed from everything that bound him" (Augustine De Pecc et Mer., 11.xxviii) nothing will delay his entrance into heaven (Trent V). Unfortunately, as the person sins, the baptismal grace is lost and there can be no return to their baptism. Grace needs to be regained through the sacrament of absolution.

Rome holds a very uncompromising position on infant baptism. Un-baptised babies are "...excluded perpetually from the vision of God . . . and deprived of the happiness of heaven" (Fanning 1996) There is no place for the remission of original sin outside of baptism and baptisms by laity are permitted to avoid the tragedy of an infant dying un-baptised. The church has not spoken authoritatively as to the state of these children though Pope Innocent III wrote that "...the punishment of original sin is the deprivation of the vision of God; of actual sin, the eternal pains of hell" (Fanning 1996). Children are not considered guilty of actual sin. Some theologians differed. Even Augustine believed they would suffer the pains of Hell (ex. Pecc Ct Mer., 1, xvi).

Rome holds that while there is only one real baptism - that of water - there are two substitutes which have the same effect, the baptism of desire and of blood. The first is simply a genuine desire but inability to be baptised. It does not preclude the need for baptism when the opportunity arises. The second is martyrdom, Matt 10:32.

The form of baptism is especially important in the Roman Catholic tradition. It must be by flowing water (no sprinkling) applied three times (in honour of the Trinity) to affect cleansing. The words must be spoken after the baptism. Provided the form is correct, it ultimately does not matter who applied it, layman, woman, even heretic or unbeliever.[19] Until Vatican II, the baptism by a heretic was of more value than one performed by a Congregational who, for instance, might utter the sacramental words prior to the water or a Methodist who only sprinkles (Fanning 1996). In such cases conditional baptism would have been conducted if the person ever became a Catholic.[20]

(b) Reformed Infant Baptism

---

[19] The validity of baptism by heretics was established during the baptismal controversy of the third century and was confirmed at Trent.
[20] In this case with the words "If thou are not yet baptised."

Calvin saw the new covenant of Christ as being a fulfilment of the covenant made with Abraham, the father of all believers. He did not attempt to defend **paedobaptism** as being a New Testament doctrine. Rather, his belief in the correctness of infant baptism was deduced from his understanding of the consequence of the continuation of the covenant relationship, equating baptism with circumcision. Calvin claimed that both were external rites corresponding to an internal regenerative work (See *Table 7)*:

"Everything that is applicable to circumcision applies also to baptism, excepting always the difference in the visible ceremony. For just as circumcision ... so now we are initiated by baptism so as to be enrolled among his people. ... Henceforth it is incontrovertible that baptism has now been substituted for circumcision and performs the same office (Institutes 4, XVI, 4).

If, in the past, God graciously made children partakers of the covenant, and the new covenant has no less grace, he must do so today (*Institutes,* 4, XVI, 5). If salvation is offered by God to the children of covenant parents why not offer them the sign of the covenant - baptism? For the Reformed Pastor his right to baptise infants does not have to be proved (Murray 1980, 50) from the New Testament, rather it is the opponents responsibility to disprove their covenantal position (Berkouwer 1969, 175). Those who oppose infant baptism are seen as claiming that the new covenant is far less gracious and encompassing than the old which had a place for children (thee and thy seed Gen 17). Should these un-baptised children die they would be doomed to hell, for only those who are in Christ have eternal life (*Institutes* 4, XVI, 17).

This is a judgement far harsher than Christ's who included infants in the kingdom of God, Matt 25.

REFORMED UNDERSTANDING OF THE CONTINUATION OF ABRAHAM'S COVENANT	
EXTERNAL ASPECTS	
Circumcision	Baptism
INTERNAL ASPECTS	
Purges from sin Dt 10:16, 30:6; Jer 4:4, 6:10, 9:25	Purges from sinActs 2:38, 22:16 1 Pet 3:21
Sets aside sinful flesh Rom 4:11, Col 2:11	Sets aside sinful flesh Rom 6:2-8; Eph 5:26
Public Testimony Gen 12:2, 46:3; Dt 4:7,6,34	Public testimony

Table 7.

While Calvin spoke of this as a believer's baptism (*Institutes*, 4, XVI, 17-20) and blurs the distinction between infant baptism and believer's baptism, he is clearer when he stated:

> "Children are baptised for future repentance and faith. Though these are not yet formed in them, yet the seed of both lies hid in them by the secret operation the Spirit" (*Institutes*, 4, XVI, 20)

It is important to see clearly that it is the faith of the parents and the church which are in operation with nothing coming from or present in the child. Baillie questioned this very issue:

> "Does this mean that the benefits of the sacraments
> come to the child in response to the faith of the
> parents and of the church? Yes, indeed; that is just
> what it means. They claim God's promise for the
> child, by faith. And that is just as it aught to be, and
> in keeping with the whole outlook of the New
> Testament, which has none of your false
> individualism." (U.D., 83)

Even if baptism is administered with correct safeguards it does not always "...follow that the administration of this rite insures for the recipient the possession of the grace signified" (Murray 1980, 51). The mysteries of God's election must be accounted for (Sasse 1985, 41-2).

(c) Lutheran Infant Baptism

While Calvin had an antipathy to anything that suggested that an action could produce a spiritual effect such as forgiveness of sins (Sasse 1985, 40), Luther had no such problems. He believed that the New Testament taught that baptism was not a sign but "the washing of regeneration" (Sasse 1985, 40), but was careful, however, not to identify the sign with the action as in *ex opere operato*. The grace of baptism is only given to a faith that is anchored to the Word and the promises of God spoken at the time of baptism. It was this Word that made baptism a sacrament, "For without the Word of God the water is simple water and no baptism.

But with the Word of God it is baptism, that is, a gracious water of life and a washing of regeneration" (SC IV). It is this association of Word and sign to make a sacrament that sets Lutheran theology apart. Luther stated that:

> "We do not agree with Thomas and the Dominicans who forget the word [God's Institution] and say that God has joined to the water a spiritual power which, through the water, washes away sin. Nor do we agree with Scotus and the Franciscans who teach that Baptism washes sin away through the assistance of the divine will, as if the washing takes place only through God's will and not at all through the Word and the Water" (Smalcald Art. III V 2-3)

THREEFOLD CONNECTION OF FAITH IN BAPTISM IN LUTHERAN TEACHING
1. Baptism is received by faith that Jesus Christ will him for his own and grant participation in his dying and living.
2. Faith is to be expected as a result of the administration of baptism just as it would be from preaching.
3. Baptism is not only the beginning but the firm abiding basis upon which faith must establish itself again and again.

Table 8.

While the faith of the parents and the church were important (LC IV 56-57) this was not the authority to baptise. For Luther, baptismal faith was not a future faith, or a seed that later awakens. The children, like the adults, come to or receives at baptism their own very real faith and the Holy Spirit is also given at that time. "Strictly speaking, even the faith of the greatest hero of the faith, even the faith of an Athanasius or Luther, is no greater than the faith of an infant" (Sasse 1985, 45). This was not a conscious faith, but Luther never associated faith with intellectual assent, rather he saw the scripture teaching that the intellect can be a stumbling block to faith (Worthing 1996).[21]   Luther had no difficulty believing that God could save an infant just as easily as an adult and saw a worthy precedent in Jesus' acceptance and use of children as an example of the Kingdom. He believed that God saw people not as infants or adults but as people who were either sons of Adam or of God.

Luther saw his walk as a lonely path between the hierarchal safeguards of Rome and the psychological safeguards of the "enthusiasts".[22] His only guide is the Word of God even when it appeared humanly impossible. Ultimately, the age of the recipient was not a real issue. He did not see justifying faith as something that happened at one moment of time but the substance of a whole life. Luther stated:

"What does such baptizing with water signify? It signifies that the Old Adam in us should, by daily contrition and repentance, be drowned and die with all sins and evil lusts and, again, a new man daily come forth and arise, who shall live before God in

[21]Worthing's audiotape on Luther's doctrine of Baptism was part of a series given by the Lutheran Church of Australia to mark the 450th anniversary of Luther's death.
[22]A term he used for the followers of Zwingli and would have applied to those of Calvin.

righteousness forever" (SC V).

For Luther, there could be no second sacrament to complete baptism, only a return to the faithfulness of God to his promises spoken at the time of baptism. While these promises could be rejected at any time "...unbelief does not then turn baptism into nothing, it remains the basis for judgement on the apostate and as power for the penitent in their battle with temptation" (Schlink 1972, 127).

(d) Zwingli's Infant Baptism

Zwingli, at first vacillated over the subject of infant baptism (Gabler 1987, 127) but eventually came down firmly on the side of infant baptism. Believing that nothing external could purify or justify, he maintained that baptism did nothing. It only testified that the baptised already belonged to God and that they would live their life accordingly (Gabler 1987, 127). His arguments for paedobaptism are similar to Calvin's - there is no prohibition in Scripture and of the continuation of Abraham's covenant in conjunction with God's election (Gabler, 1987, 129).

The Zurich reformer's contribution to the understanding of baptism is extremely important. Unwillingly, he sowed the seeds of the **Anabaptist** movement which developed in that city during his lifetime. It would include some of his most dedicated followers (Estep 1986, 11). They drew on his understanding of the church being a congregation of the faithful (Gebler 1985, 125) and of baptism being a symbol only. They also reacted against Zwingli, believing he had not gone far enough in his reforms.

Believers Baptism [23]

The most provocative act of the reformation that symbolized the break from Rome was the re-baptism as believers of a group of Christians in Zurich on January 21, 1525 (Estep 1986,11-12). The Anabaptists were not just a product of the Reformation. Cardinal Hosius, the president of the Council of Trent, said, "...Were it not that the baptists have been grievously tormented and cut off with the knife during the past 1200 year, they would swarm in greater numbers today than all the reformers" (Hoad 1986, 5) The defence of paedobaptism by Baille of appealing to practice of the great churches (U.D. ??) is no longer adequate, as this form of baptism, opposed to the death by Catholics and Protestants alike, is set to eventually become the predominate form of baptism of church attenders.[24]

There is more to being a Baptistic church than a common mode of baptism. The sacrament (or *ordinance* as Baptists prefer) must be viewed in a context of their doctrine of the church which is not in submission to the state and a high view of scripture which frees

---

[23]It is difficult to give a title to the Baptist practice as some paedobaptists claim theirs is a believers baptism while Baptists will baptise children where there is evidence of conversion so it cannot be called adult baptism. The writer acknowledges the inadequacy of this term. The Baptists often use the term *Christian baptism* but to use it requires making a judgement before the facts are assessed.

[24]Already in Australia, there are more Pentecostals in church than in the Uniting church and to this number must be added the Baptists and Church of Christ.

them from what they believe to be pre-reformation errors. They stress personal repentance, faith in Christ and voluntary commencement of discipleship in baptism (Hoad 1986, 16). Baptist theology tends to be very simple, baptism means immersion and its recipients are those to whom the gospel has been preached, Matt. 28:19, and who are regenerate, Acts 2. Perhaps, it is this simplicity that caused paedobaptist theologians to ignore their claims but they were forced to face the issue when Karl Bath, one of the 20th century's foremost theologians took the Baptist position (Berkouwer 1969, 161).

Baptists rejected (Hoad 1986, 279) the belief of a church visible and invisible (West. Conf. Ch 25 Sect 2) insisting instead that the church was a company of regenerate persons gathered by God in a given locality. Its members have given evidence of spiritual life by their own repentance and faith in Christ. They have begun a voluntary yet indissoluble discipleship by believers baptism. Baptists are not an homogenous group, compriseing three main groupings - general, particular and American - with differing theologies of salvation.

Baptists generally see the sacraments as an act of obedience to the gospel of Christ as symbolized in the sacrament and would follow Zwingli in not seeing them as an access to any saving grace (Hoad, 1985, 237). Baptism is, however, full of grace for many Baptists. It can be a joyful acceptance of the saving grace already received (Beasley-Murray, 1992, 19) and as a focus for the grace required for daily living as a Christian.

Discussion

The Jewish practice of baptising proselytes, a precursor to Christian baptism, involved the baptism of the whole family including infants (Sasse 1985, 38) and there is strong evidence that the early church baptised babies. It is spoken of by Iranaeus (Adv Haer: 2:22.4) in a manner that indicates that there was no controversy. When Polycarp spoke of serving his Lord for 86 years (Stevenson 1970, 21) it is difficult to see it as other than his inclusion into the church. This dates his baptism prior to AD 70, the apostolic period. The first known objection to the practice is by Tertullian who does not view it as an innovation. It appears that both practices existed side by side. For the Catholic, there is value in a reference to the practice of the church fathers but to the Protestant, as the Lutheran scholar Sasse (1985, 39) points out, it does not decide the theological question of infant baptism. It could have been an ancient misuse, as was the baptism of the dead. The theological issue must be decided by Scripture only and the evidence from apostolic practice is ambiguous. Calvin correctly stated:

> "We nowhere read of even one infant having being baptised by the hands of the apostles. For although this is not expressly narrated by the Evangelists, yet ... they are not expressly excluded when mention is made of any baptised family" *(Institutes 4.16.8)*

FAMILY BAPTISMS	
Acts 10	Cornelius - all who were baptised received the Holy Spirit
Acts 16	Lydia - Her home was composed of "brothers".
Acts 16	Jailor - All baptised were filled with joy.
Acts 18	Crispus - All who were believed were baptised
1 Cor. 1	Stephanus - All who were baptised were serving the Lord c.f. 1 Cor. 16:15

Table 9.

The reformed position stands or falls on one point only, that of equating baptism and circumcision (Berkouwer 1969, 164&170). By having already decided that the children of Christians are already saved, they are obligated to reject Baptist proof texts. We can even find in Calvin the very un-Protestant defence of tradition (*Institutes* 4,16.8). Calvin is correct in seeing a continuity between the new covenant of Jesus and the covenant to Abraham[25] but he went too far when he deduced equivalence from the similarities between baptism and circumcision. The doctrine of the faithful remnant,1 Kings 20:18; Ezek. 6:8, 14:22, teaches that the Old Testament sacrament did not make a true people of the Spirit, Rom. 9:6-8. Both Testaments are agreed that mere circumcision and descent from Abraham does not cause a person to be saved. Abraham was justified by God given faith, Gen. 15:6, Rom. 4:1-4, and since that time, the just have lived by their God given faith. Hab. 2:4.

---

[25]Refer to my essay, *The God of Isaac,* a discussion of Old Testament grace.

It is difficult to see any practical difference between the view of Zwingli and Calvin, for in both, baptism offers nothing that was not there before baptism. Their necessity of baptism comes from Christ's command.

For Luther, there is a necessity of means as "...it works forgiveness of sins, delivers from death and the Devil, and gives eternal salvation to all who believe this, as the words and promises of God declare" (SC IV). He was correct in seeing faith as entirely separate from intellectual assent. He was also correct in refusing to separate the individual's faith and baptism. His belief that children have faith is impossible to prove, but the example of John the Baptist does show that spiritual response can start even in the womb.

The Presbyterian, Baille, unwittingly put a strong case for immersion when he says "... the most characteristic teaching about baptism in the New Testament appears to be closely connected with the symbolism of baptism by immersion . . . What rich and unforgettable symbolism of putting off the old man and putting on the new! And after all symbolism is a vital part of any sacrament (U.D., 74). He went on to say that "...In the New Testament baptism seems regularly to mean the baptism of grown men and women who have heard the gospel and have received it with personal faith and now take the deliberate conscious step of entering into the Church of Christ" (U.D., 74-5). He conceded that immersion has the most powerful psychological effect on the baptised and the congregation but warned that "...a powerful psychological effect at the time" can be very dangerous as it is faith and intent that counts (U.D., 80). More important than the psychological effect or the quality of the faith and intent is a conscious encounter with the grace of God.

It is generally agreed the New Testament teaches that one becomes a member of the visible church, not by decision or by birth but through baptism. Baptism is indispensably linked to salvation and church membership but the nature of this link is expressed in widely divergent terms. It would appear difficult to find any common ground, especially when we consider the strong and authoritative denunciation of Protestant views at Trent. With the Protestant Church strongly founded in *sola scriptura* and *sola fide* it would appear that it could not harmonize its views with Rome except through abandoning its Protestant distinctives. There is also the question of how much common ground exists within the various practices of Protestantism. The Baptist and Lutheran practices are addressed below to highlight variations in the protestant traditions.

While portraying baptism as representing something already accomplished, the Baptist would generally see baptism as sign of grace. The Baptist sees salvation as coming through repentance from dead works and faith towards God. This is something a child cannot do and it would therefore follow that the child is doomed to hell fire, in line with Augustine's view. It is, however, uncommon to see a Baptist who is prepared to tell grieving Christian parents that their infant is eternally lost (Beasley-Murray 1992, 20) . In such a case the Baptist would often appeal to the very same scriptures that the paedobapists do, for example Matt 21:16. The significance is seldom recognized by Baptists themselves (Steere Pers. Com. 1997). It means that they are holding two quite distinct doctrines[26] of salvation simultaneously and could well be accused of inconsistency.[27]

It is difficult to speak against the validity of a true reception of grace by a Lutheran who had been baptised as a child and, who from an early age, daily returned to his baptism and through faith in God's promise daily buries his "old man" to live in newness of life. Unfortunately, this is not always the outcome of paedobaptism especially where there is a strong belief that the infant is already a Christian.[28] There is often no attempt to bring that person to a crisis of faith. Too often faith never grows and the person drifts away. The Lutheran, Montgomery described the church as a place where men hear God's call and become saints. He stated that outside of a personal meeting with Christ the church only holds damnation (1970, 85-93)

The scriptures seem to teach against a simplistic doctrine of salvation operating along a narrow unbending path. It is possibly not coincidental that Baptist practice is flourishing in the west in a time of low infant mortality whereas the paedobaptist practice stems from an age of distressingly high infant mortality. These different ages required a different emphasis in pastoral theology. There is an implicit belief throughout the church that children can

---

[26]If this is only a hope, as the writer has often heard it expressed, and not a doctrine the pastor could well be offering a false hope.

[27]When discussing this point with Rev. Steere, a Baptist pastor with approximately 30 years experience in the Particular Baptist tradition, he commented that they did proclaim a message of gracious acceptance to the families on the death of unrepentant and un-baptised babies. He had only once read where a Baptist acknowledged a dual doctrine. He commented that the logic is hard to refute.

[28]The writer spent his first 20 years in a paedobaptist denomination and never once heard that his sin was an affront to a holy God. Sinners were those outside the church. I expect that this is not an uncommon experience.

be saved. If they cannot be saved, Christianity can only be a message of despair for many families, instead of a glorious gospel of grace.

6 THE EUCHARIST

With baptism there were points of strong contention between the arms of the church. The eucharist was to prove an even greater cause of division. The major views will be considered in turn.

The Sacrifice of the Mass

It is possibly the Mass more than any other doctrine that divides Rome from Protestantism. The word *Mass* is derived from the Latin, *Missio*, a dismissal, in the sense of "close of prayer". A balanced understanding of the Mass requires that it be viewed pre and post Vatican 2.

Pre Vatican 2

Anglicans have been known to speak of the eucharist as a sacrifice as it involves a sacrifice of praise - pleading the sacrifice of Christ's death and the sacrifice of ourselves (Renfrey 1976, 67).

The Catholic recognizes and values these internal sacrifices, Psm 1:18, 26:6, 111:2, but believes their very validity presupposes a real, true and continuing sacrifice. Without a continuing sacrifice which derives its value from the cross, Christianity, which should be the perfect religion, would be inferior not only to the Old Covenant but also the poorest form of natural religion (Phole, 1996). As the scriptures will not permit this sacrifice to be either new or complimentary, the Mass can be nothing other than the same sacrifice (Phole, 1996). A valid sacrifice requires that something be destroyed or literally transformed at a designated place by a priest. Any less an understanding warrants an anathema (Trent, 22.1).

Rome draws heavily on the Old Testament for its scriptural proof. Melchezidec, whose priesthood was a type of Christ's, Psm 109:4 Heb 5:5, brought gifts of bread and wine, Gen 14:18-20. The type resembles the anti-type not in the cross but at the last supper. This was where, it is believed, Christ made an un-bloody oblation of his body and blood, in the same manner the priest does now in the Mass, "...According to the unanimous interpretation of the fathers" (Phole 1996). Malachi 1:10-11 speaks clearly of the abolition and replacement of the Levitical sacrifices with a new sacrifice. The Hebrew word for sacrifice indicates that the new sacrifice will also be a real sacrifice. This sacrifice cannot be Golgotha, as Malachi's prophecy requires that it be performed worldwide among the Gentiles by priests. The sacrifice at the altar of Christ, Heb. 6:4ff, speaks of the time Christ foretold saying that men would worship in spirit and truth, John 4:21ff. Christ's own words of institution, Luke 22:20, I Cor 11:25, are clearly said to prove that the sacrifice of **expiation** took place at the Last Supper, not Calvary. This is because the chalice not the cross inaugurated the New Testament. The separate consecration and **transubstantiation** of wine and bread to blood and body show the elements mystical separation as in his death. This involved a metaphysical change that could not be perceived by the senses, which allowed God to be in heaven and on the altar at the same time (Matros, 1981, 272).

The Mass actually comprises two portions, a sacrament and sacrifice. It is a sacrament in that it serves as a representation and commemoration (Trent, 22,1), and it sanctifies the soul by applying to the individual the fruits of the Sacrifice of the Cross by simple distribution. The application of the true and proper sacrifice, which glorifies God through adoration, works as a *specific offering* (Trent 22,1). As a "specific offering", it can benefit not only the recipient but also the living and the dead for sins, punishments, satisfactions and other necessities (Trent 22, Can. 3). Prayers said at the time of the sacrifice will propitiate the merciful God for those who are gone before us (Cyril of Jerusalem Catech. Myst v,.8).

The old order had sacrifices of praise, thanksgiving, propitiation and **impetration,** Lev 4, 2 Kings 21, and, it is argued, the better sacrifice should also. The God-ward effect of the Mass is adoration and thanksgiving, and towards man the fruit of the Mass is **impetration** and **expiation**. The value of the Mass is limitless but humanity is incapable of converting it into an infinite effect on their souls. Its effectiveness will "...depend very much on the personal efforts and worthiness, the devotion and fervour of those who celebrate or are present at the Mass. . . . [and that] from the unlimited treasure of the Mass much more grace will result to the individual from a service participated in by a full congregation"

(Phole 1996). In this sense, the special fruits are obtained *ex opere operantus*.

Instead of public worship the Mass developed into clerical prayer with some churches having up to 100 priests employed only to say the Mass (Matros 1981, 278) which was most frequently performed privately by the priest for a fee. Too frequently the laity would be discouraged from partaking because of their sinfulness and the practice developed of the priest holding the host high so that it could be worshipped. The Mass became burdened with superstition and excessive ritual, even to the placement of hands and fingers and the pronunciation of words. For 1000 years, the faithful would have to wait to understand and follow what the priest was doing, as the Mass was only said in Latin. They had to be content with saying their rosary during Mass (Matros 1981, 293-4). Catholics will readily agree that there was much superstition associated with the Mass and that the Church needed to be reformed. Some would say that this reformation did not start seriously to occur until Vatican 2 (Taylor *Pers. Com.* 1997).

Despite the errors ((Matros 1981, 293) Rome held a strong individualistic expectation that in the Mass "a Catholic could in fact experience themselves as present at Christ's sacrifice an the cross and feel its redemptive graces flooding their hearts" (Matros 1981, 291-2)

Post Vatican 2

The Mass, which was so strongly objected to by the reformers is all but gone. While Rome does not officially disown the doctrines of Trent, she now gives them different "empthasis" (Pers. Com., Taylor, 1997). The real effect is that "Catholicism in general is quietly laying them aside" (Matros,1981, 293). Matros, a modern Catholic theologian, claimed that the term *Transubstantiation* is virtually unknown to young Catholics and her theologians no longer refer to the Mass as a sacrifice. The very word *Mass,* so hated by the reformers, is disappearing from theological usage (1981, 192-3).

SUMMARY OF CHANGES TO THE MASS	
Pre Vatican 2	Post Vatican 2
Watched from a distance	Expected to Participate
A silent ritual	Little silence
A sacrifice in which few participated	A eucharist in which most partake
Priest offers privately with back to the people	Priest faces the people and leads in worship
Priest's preaching role limited	Priest's preaching role greatly expanded
Preparation was cursory because of set liturgy	Service is expected to have ceremonial variety
A private experience	Public worship
Liturgy was in Latin	Liturgy in the vernacular
Theology basis was fixed at Trent	New directions in theology
Scholastic understanding	Scriptural understanding
The sacrament is worshipped	The entire liturgy is an act of worship

Table 10.

The growth for liturgical reform grew initially from the 19th century Benedictine monks doing research into the prayers incorporated in the Tridentine liturgy. They discovered that the liturgy of the early Middle Ages (especially under Pope Gregory) was different from their liturgy in that the laity were expected to participate. It also differed in that the old emphasis of the Mass was a communal, not private, experience. Though translations of the liturgy were first made in the 1880's these were not legally sanctioned untill 1897. Gradually the movement gained more supporters and increased participation by the laity was allowed. Further research carried out between the world wars, most notably by Jungmann and Dix (Matros 1981, 294) showed conclusively that in many ways Trent was out of step with tradition. Pope John 23rd called the second Vatican Council in 1959, charging it with updating the church through a *Constitution on the Sacred Liturgy* (Matros 1981, 295). Changes were so rapid during the 60's and 70's some laity barely knew what to expect when they went to church (Matros 1981, 296). For the layman the changes could not be more complete, though the full impact of Vatican 2 will take some time to filter through to the church worldwide (Pers. Com., Taylor, 1997).

Theological changes are developing following these radical changes of practice but where these will lead is uncertain. Matros, speaking of these changes said:

> "During the past twenty years, then, Catholic Theology has been explicitly attempting to recover the patristic and scriptural understanding of the Eucharist and to translate it into terms that make sense to people today. By and Large it is

abandoning the Tridentine insistence on transubstantiation and on the mass as a sacrifice in favour of other interpretations which are equally Catholic but less scholastic. And in doing this it is shifting its attention from the blessed sacrament as an object of worship to the entire liturgy as an act of worship." (Matros 1981, 301)

Consubstantiation

In the 1200s there were three views as to how the bread and wine became the body and blood of Christ. *Transubstantiation* has already been discussed. A second view, *annihilism* was a succession of realities in which the body and blood annihilated the bread and wine. A third view, called *consubstantiation,* held that the body and blood were added to the bread and wine when the words of consecration were spoken. Annihilation and consubstantiation had only limited acceptance in Catholicism and were considered heretical after 1250 (Matros 1981, 271). Rome rejected them on philosophical grounds as they were either implausible or too miraculous.

Consubstantiation is often said to be the doctrinal position of the Lutherans (Thomas, 1963, 397) a claim Lutherans strenuously deny (Schmidt 1961, 571). This misunderstanding possibly came about by combining Luther's doctrine of "the right hand of God"[29]

---

[29]The resurrected Jesus is said to be at the right hand of God (1 Peter 3:22). Luther asked where this is, was he only "up there" in heaven as Zwingli would say? Luther reasoned that as God is omnipresent, Christ's presence must also be omnipresent and therefore in the elements as he would be in the leaves of a tree. This general

with a very loose understanding of consubstantiation.

Precursors of Change

Long before Luther nailed his 95 thesis on the castle church door at Wittenberg in 1517 there were moves afoot for the reform of the church which could not be restrained forever. Wycliffe (c1330-1384) had denounced transubstantiation in his works *On Apostasy* and the *On the Eucharist* in 1379 and 1380 and was not burned as an apostate. The Bohemian, John Hus (c1370-1415) was greatly influenced by Wycliffe and though he was burnt at the stake for holding many of Wycliffe's views a movement was set in place in his native Bohemia which would be more radical than that of Huss. The *Four Articles of Prague* (1420) demanded:

1. Freedom throughout Bohemia for preaching God's word

2. There should be communion in both bread and wine for all

3. The clergy should abandon riches and **simony**

4. The clergy and laity should free themselves from all mortal and venial sins

Four bloody wars ensued between 1421 and 1427 and following the inability of the papal forces to subdue Bohemia, agreement was

---

presence did not guarantee that Christ was in every circumstance to our benefit. There were places Christ wanted to be found.

reached in 1436 where Bohemia was allowed to keep the first two articles and a previously heretical movement was accepted as legitimate. The way was now open for the later reformers who would assault the papal government of the church (Packer 1965, 90).

The papacy would be responsible for bringing on the reformation by its own actions. The spiritual state of most of the church at the time of the reformation was very sad. Medieval man had little fear of the flames of hell. He was after all baptised and, provided he died after being forgiven by the priest he had no likelihood of going to hell. As only the pure could go to heaven, for many there would be a period of purifying in the temporary but severe pains of purgatory. "This was a very real place to medieval man and filled him with dread. The church kept him aware of his sin and its consequences, qualitatively with an intensity that portrayed it as diabolical, and quantitatively with such enormous time spans as to make time kiss eternity"[30] (Atkinson, 1968, 141). In the early church there was a practice of indulgences to deal with lapses into sin which was public confession before the congregation and repentance. This degenerated into private confession to the priest and suitable penance and eventually a cash payment (Atkinson, 1968, 142). By 1030, French bishops offered a partial remission of purgatory for some meritorious act and eventually in 1063 full remissions were offered to those who died in a war against Islam and in 1187 for someone who paid for a soldier to fight against Islam. The practice would degenerate further until what was once a spiritual activity degenerated into a "holy trade" concentrated in the hands of the Pope and indulgences would be given to anyone alive or dead who could pay for them (or have them paid for).

---

[30]The relics in the castle church where Luther nailed his theses to the door were reputed to earn a remission of 1,902,202 years, 270 days (Atkinson, 1968, 147)

There was now no longer any need for faith in Christ, God's forgiveness or assurance of salvation. When Pope Leo X decided to build St. Peters at Rome he used the flagrant use of indulgences to do it.[31] Tetzel, the Dominican chosen to do the job would say:

> "The dead cry, "pity us! Pity us! We are in dire torment from which you can redeem us for a pittance .... Will you leave us here in flames? Will you delay our promised glory?
>
>> As soon as a coin in the coffer rings
>> The soul from purgatory springs
>
> Will you not then for a mere quarter of a florin receive these letters of indulgence through which you are able to lead a divine and immortal soul into the fatherland of paradise?" (Atkinson, 1968, 149)

For Martin Luther this was too much, the church was apostate, held in the sway of anti-Christ.

Lutheran Communion

The document on which the reformation was founded, Luther's

---

[31]The amounts of money involved were astronomical, as were the indulgences offered. Tetzel's wage was 20 times that of a university professor, he offered full remission of sins, the penitent could chose his own confessor, they would participate in the merits of the saints and, they would relieve the poor suffering in purgatory. (Atkinson, 1968, 148)

ninety five theses, "differed from the ordinary propositions for debate because they were forged in anger. The ninety five affirmations are crisp, bold unqualified" (Bainton, 1978, 60), Luther was driven by his love of the truth and his revulsion at the state of the church which climaxed in the sale of indulgences (Atkinson, 1968, 150).[32] When he nailed his theses to the castle church door in Wittenberg he chose all saints day 1517, to show his connection with, not rejection of the rich heritage of the church. Luther was conscious of the need to preserve that part of the Catholic heritage which was scriptural while ridding it of practices rooted only in tradition; this made him the most conservative of the reformers. When Luther did change from the Roman church, he only slowly gave up each point. Of all his reforms, Luther knew that communion would involve the greatest battle and require the enormous faith for here the battle was drawn between the tradition of the church and *sola fide* (WA 6,512). There were already stirrings over the Lord 's Supper in the 95 theses (conclusion 7) and by 1518 Luther had rejected *ex opere operato* believing that divine grace must precede the sacrament though he never denied their objective nature. In 1520 in his *Treatise on the New Testament* he abandoned the belief of the mass as a sacrifice.

Sasse stated Luther's position as "...the sacraments do not create faith; they are rather accepted as by faith, and serve as acts of God, to assure the faithful of God's grace (1977, 67). They did not guarantee a gracious God. The discoverer of *sola gratia* knew that there could be no synergism between God and humanity as we

---

[32]Luther's stand on Indulgences was not just the rebellion of a nationalistic German against the greedy Italians as the university where he was a professor and the castle church was supported by indulgences. He was driven by his responsibility as a priest towards his parishioners, noe matter what the personal cost was (Bainton, 1978, 55-6).

brought nothing to the sacraments[33] but rather received freely from the hand of God. Luther said:

> "We must let the mass be a sacrament and a testament, and this is not and cannot be a sacrifice . . . We should, therefore, give careful heed to this word "sacrifice" that we do not presume to give God something in the sacrament when it is he who gives us all things" (WA 6, 231).

Luther believed that the Mass as a sacrifice was a real manifestation of the Anti-Christ (Sasse 1977, 69), however his books show he retained an unswerving belief in the real presence of Christ in the Lord's Supper. Because of this belief, he did not see transubstantiation as a great sin but only as a poor "opinion" (Sasse 1977, 80, 82) of what occurred. His belief in the real presence was held only after a deep inner struggle.   In a letter to the Christians of Strasbourg he wrote:

> "That I admit: if Dr. Carlstadt or someone else had told me five years ago that in the sacrament there is nothing but mere bread and mere wine, he would have rendered me a great service. I passed through great inner struggles in that respect . . . For I was well aware that by these means I could strike the hardest blow against Rome. . . . But I am captured by the words of God and cannot find a way out.

---

[33]This was in contrast to the mass of his day which said: "Grant that the sacrifice which I, though unworthy, have offered in the sight of Thy majesty may be acceptable to Thee and through Thy mercy be a propitiation for me and for all those for whom I have offered it up." (Sasse 1977, 70).

> The words are there, and they are too strong for me.
> Human words cannot take them out of my soul[34]."
> (WA 15, 394)

Evangelical freedom was always Luther's approach to communion, understanding it to be a gift of the gospel. This was in sharp contrast to the Bohemians who saw Christ as a new Moses and the Mass as an ordinance of the new law which had to be observed to the letter. Luther believed that the legalistic attitude behind the bloodshed in the Bohemian's argument with Rome, did not manifest the gospel and was as wrong as the tyrants who had denied the two elements to the people.[35] These were minor things that should have been settled by a general Council of the Church. A legalistic approach to the sacrament stood in the way of a Saviour who wanted to give the grace of salvation through it (Sasse 1977, 76).

FOUR ERRORS LUTHER SAID MUST BE REJECTED IN THE LORD'S SUPPER
1. That only bread and wine are present
2. Giving the words of institution a spiritual meaning, i.e. Being incorporated into my spiritual body
3. The bread does not remain in the sacrament (a small error)
4. The mass is a sacrifice and good work

Table 11 (Sasse, 1977, 83-4)

---

[34]This period of doubting is dated at 1519 prior to writing his *Treatise on the Blessed Sacrament of the Holy and True Blood of Christ and on Fraternities* which do not show any indication of the turmoil he spoke of.

[35]This occurred at the Decree of Constance in 1415.

Luther described the essential nature of the Lord's Supper saying, "The sacrament of the Altar is the true body and blood of our Lord Jesus Christ, in and under bread and wine, instituted and commanded by the word of Christ to be eaten and drunk by us Christians."(L C,V.8). He would not countenance any thought of a Zwinglian metaphorical interpretation, being certain that Christ was speaking literally when he said "this **is** my body." The common Lutheran expression "*In with and under the bread*" are carefully chosen words to repudiate any connection with transubstantiation while at the same time affirming "... the sacramental union of the substance of the unchanged bread with the body of Christ" (Schmidt 1961, 559).

DIFFERENT FORMS OF CHRIST'S PRESENCE IN LUTHERANISM
1. Physically present and comprehensible as when he was on earth
2. Physically present in an incomprehensible way as with the resurrection body which could penetrate solid walls (this is sacramental presence)
3. Present anywhere through his omnipotence

Table 12. (Schmidt, 1961, P562-3)

For Luther, Christ had become flesh and dwelt among us and continues to dwell among us in the sacrament. His views about the real presence are often presented as *consubstantiation*[36] but

---

[36]Sasse (1977. 81) claims that the confusion came about through an English translation of a Latin translation of a passage in the original German work, *Book of Concord* (Form. Conc. Sol. Decl 7.37). In that book Luther comments on his surprise at learning while reading comments on transubstantiation made by Peter d' Ailly (who favoured consubstantiation) that it was only a theory. As a theory it

nowhere did he accept consubstantiation nor has the church officially done so.[37] He would not express his opinion in one of the philosophical frameworks of the Catholic scholastics. He held the doctrine of the real presence without trying to explain it, as it simply defied human explanation:

> We care nothing about the philosophical subtlety by which they teach bread and wine leave or loose their own natural substance, and that there remains only the appearance and colour of bread, and not true bread. For it is in perfect agreement with Holy Scriptures that there is, and remains, bread, as Paul himself calls it, 1 Cor. 11:28 "The bread which we break". And 1 Cor 11:28 "let him so eat of that bread" (Smalcald Art. Part III, Article VI)

Luther was no Deist as he argued that Christ's body cannot only be localized in heaven. Christ was at the right hand of the Father who was unrestingly active in all his creation. As God was omnipresent, Christ was also present in all things. But his presence at the communion was different to his general presence as it was there for our benefit. If Christ was not present his grace would not be present and there would be "... no longer a manifest sign of the presence of the true and gracious God . . . among men" (Watson 1966, 163). As it was Christ's nature to help when he was in the flesh, so in the sacrament, the believer can look to the again present Christ for healing, both physical and spiritual (Althaus 1966, 394).

---

could never become doctrine no matter how many Popes or councils ratified it. He did not however support consubstantiation in that passage.

[37]No doubt some pastors in the Lutheran church have held this view but this individual freedom must be separated from the normal position.

Christ's presence can be experienced in two equal ways - sacramentally and spiritually - through communion and when in faith the gospel is heard and meditated on (Form Conc Sol. Dec, 7:61). This second eating of his body is described as *Capernaitic manducation*, (John 6). This does not do away with the need for the sacrament as it depends on the recipient's willingness to accept this same grace through the sacraments (Watson 1966, 164).

Zwingli's Communion

Zwingli, though a contemporary of Luther, was as anxious to rid the church of tradition as Luther was to retain what was good. He rid his churches of paintings, crosses, organs and choirs (Rilliet, 1964 218). Up to 1525, there was little separating Zwingli from Luther and other reformers on the Lords Supper. He had already denied that the Mass cleanses from sin in 1522, and in his *Concluding Statements* of 1523, denounced the Mass as a sacrifice. In 1524, Andreas Carlstadt published three pamphlets[38] denouncing the real presence of Christ in the sacrament and in that same year, Zwingli also adopted it.[39] His reasoning for interpreting **"is"** figuratively in the words of institution were based on a treatise by the Dutch humanist Cornelius Hoehn[40] (Sasse 1977, 97).

---

[38] Rilliet (1964, 222-3) suggests that the prompting behind these works was more due to personal rivalry and ill-will towards Luther than a deep spiritual conviction.

[39] There were a number of pamphlets published in 1524-5 where he rejected the real presence,. These were really debates with Luther

[40] In this thesis he likened the sacrament to a wedding ring (Sasse 1977, P98)

The Zurich reformer put his clearest argument against the real presence in the sacrament. In his 1526 book *A Clear Briefing about Christ's Supper*. These were:

1. If Christ's blood and body were present it could be seen;

2. On the basis of John 6:63 he was certain that only spiritual things gave spiritual life while the physical gave nothing. The words of institution and the elements are a parable pointing away from themselves to a higher, salvation bringing reality, but could themselves never bring it;

3. The divine and human natures of Christ are sharply separated and no fusion occurs. Because Christ now has a human body and is at God's right hand he cannot be present in the eucharist,[41] John 14:3; and

4. In sharing communion the congregation pledges to follow Christ after confessing their faith and contemplating the work of Christ (Gabler 1987, 135)

The key elements of Zwingli's communion were giving thanks, coming together, confessing and pledging (Gabler 1987, 135). In his explicit activism, Zwingli is diametrically opposed to Luther, for the sacrament was not God giving but us giving to God (Althaus 1966, 392). Zwingli wanted to avoid the possibility of two forms of salvation - the cross of Christ and the sacraments (Rilliet 1964, 228). Though denying the real presence, he did not deny that the gift of salvation was present. This presence, however, was in the heart of the communicant as he responded

---

[41]This is a denial of the doctrine of ubiquity.

with gratitude. Because of this, he preferred the term *act of thanksgiving* instead of sacrament (Gabler 1987, 134).The elements had a supporting role in building faith as the communicant contemplated Christ's sufferings but they never created it. The Passover was seen as giving guidance to the symbolic understanding. There, he claimed, it was not the lamb that was important but the remembering.

Luther considered this teaching more dangerous than that of the Pope's. If all the blessings of the sacrament could be gained spiritually, it made the sacrament redundant (Sasse 1977, 98). His preoccupation with the debate possibly blinded both reformers to the growing desire for retribution brewing amongst the Catholics. Philip of Hess wanted to present a vast protestant front from Byrne through Saxony to Brandenburg but unity of the theologians would be necessary (Rilliet 1964, 242-5) The two reformers met at Marburg in 1529 to discuss the matter but without reaching agreement.[42]

Assessment

Clearly, many of the church fathers did talk in very strong terms of "eating the body and blood of Christ" while others denounced it. Others, including Augustine and Ignatius, appear to contradict

---

[42]The articles of Marburg showed, that despite disagreement on the real presence there was remarkable unity among the Protestants including trinity, incarnation, unity of two natures of Christ, original sin, redemption by faith in Christ's sufferings the nature of faith, the futility of works and merit as well as monastic vows, the Holy spirit, baptism, confession and the renunciation of human tradition. (Rilliet, 1964, 265)

themselves suggesting that much of the strong rhetoric of the Church fathers fathers should be taken as exaggerated Oriental Symbolism. No clear unified picture can be drawn from tradition and the verdict that Rome itself is now in the process of diluting the doctrine of Mass as sacrifice and transubstantiation, should be a sufficient basis for the rejection of these doctrines.

When Zwingli talks of the many blessings that are received spiritually, such as: remembrance; pledging loyalty; coming together as a people of faith; and as a testimony to the world he is correct. Luther himself spoke like this. The issue to be resolved is, however, are the words of institution when Jesus said "this *is* my Body". Did he mean "this *represents* my body"? This determines whether we are dealing with Christ's re-presenting of himself or a naked sign - that is a powerful means of grace or a signpost to where that grace may be found? Clearly Zwingli is wrong when he rejects the value of anything which is not a spiritual exercise and done in the flesh for Christ came in the flesh, born of a virgin, dwelt among us and, in his flesh, received the penalty that was ours. Satan was conquered through Christ's flesh. He is also wrong when he denounces the doctrine of **ubiquity**. Christ is certainly at the right hand of God but he also dwells in each believer in his fullness, Eph 3:17, and we in him, John 4:13, without multiplication or diminution. He promised to be with us to the end. To place Christ only "up there" makes him less accessible. Zwingli appears to present an unbiblical dualism of spirit and flesh. Luther is correct in seeing sinfulness as being the opposite of the spirit.

Christ did speak in parables which, at the same time, concealed and revealed truth. However almost the last thing he told his disciples before his death was that the time of speaking in parables to those who love him had ended, John 16:25-29. Zwingli would leave us with a parable. Luther, on the other hand, gives us Christ, his body again in the hands of humanity to do with as they please to be received in faith for their salvation or, in disbelief to damnation. The words of inception have often been put aside lightly as it was believed that to accept them was to give tacit approval to Rome and the old philosophical positions of a physical presence. This is not the case. The real presence can be accepted as a valid Protestant position in no way similar to old Catholicism. The words of Scripture favour Luther and, when the sacrament is taken in faith relying only on the grace of God, the believer truly communes with the risen Lord. There he/she finds all the blessings of salvation refreshed to his Spirit..

Zwingli admitted that Luther may have had the words of the gospel in his favour but that he had its spirit. In doing so, however, he appears to reduce his theology to the limit of human understanding. While Luther was aware that there may be some uncertainty about the meaning of the words *"this is my body"* he would not let human reason be the final judge of the words God had spoken Himself:

> "If we must have an uncertain text and interpretation, I would rather one from the mouth of God himself than one spoken by men. And if I must be deceived, I would rather be deceived by God (if that were possible) than by men. For if God deceives me, he will take the responsibility but men cannot make amends to me if they have deceived me and led me into hell" (WA 26 446).

The choice between form and substance ultimately rests on an attitude that judges the scripture or is judged by it.

7 ADMINISTERING THE SACRAMENTS

Article 26 of the 39 articles of the Church of England states the unworthiness of the minister does not hinders the effect of the sacraments. It is very realistic about the state the ministry can be lowered to, saying "... although in the visible Church the evil be ever mingled with the good, and sometimes the evil have chief authority in the ministration of the word and sacrament." This article not only dealt with the gross abuses of the Papacy but the ministry in the local parish. Thomas (1963, 368) speaks of the time of writing the article when "...The scandal was great in the eyes of many to find the law depriving them of the ministers they trusted, and commanding them to attend the Parish Church, served perhaps by a man who had conformed to every change of Henry, Edward, Mary and Elizabeth, and whose morals and learning they held equally cheap." The Arzburg Confession also followed the same line in Article 28.

These confessions had the effect of not "unchurching" anyone and exhibited charity towards other Churches. It was not suggested that it was tolerable to receive the sacraments from people living in gross sin but at times this was forced upon the faithful by government laws and also at times in ignorance of the ministers sin. The issue was, how much did the validity of the sacrament depend on the spiritual state of the minister. At the time of the reformation there were a number of radical sects including elements of the Anabaptists which maintained that the sacraments were only valid when administered by worthy men. This had the effect of denying salvation to those outside of their own group because after all, if the minister was holy and seeking truth he would be one of us.

This was not a new issue, Tertullian said that heretics did not administer the sacraments because they worshipped a different god. Cyprian and other African Bishops also denied the validity of baptism by heretics and schismatics as it is a "... baptism into another Gospel" and "... begat children to the Devil and not to God." (Thomas 1963, 367-8). These views would be completely over-ridden by the church when it had to deal with the Donatists in the 4th century.[43] While the Donatists would not accept baptisms performed by the church, the church accepted baptisms performed by the Donatists. Augustine taught that the grace associated with the ministerial role was not dependant on the spirituality of the person who administers it. In hearing and receiving from the minister the believer hears and receives from God (Luke 10:16).

The issue was whether the sacraments were a gift from God himself to the recipient and not dependant on the minister, or was it a gift from a particular church given by a man who was set aside for the task because of his qualifications. If the validity of the sacrament was dependant on the minister there could, ultimately,

---

[43] The Donatists broke with the north African church because they believed the Bishop of Carthage had committed a deadly sin in failing to maintain his witness under persecution and so, it was claimed, could not convey the grace of ordination. They re-baptised all who came to their group.

be no guarantee of the effectiveness of the sacraments as no man truly knows the heart and spirituality of the minister. If it is dependent on God's faithfulness there could never be any doubt about its effectiveness because he had proven himself eternally faithful at the cross. If the sacraments are a gift of the church there is a ground for denominational baptism, a division among the visible church, which Paul condemned in 1 Corinthians. While there can be disputes about the validity of a form of baptism, the reality is there is only Christian baptism, never a denominational baptism.

Paul spoke of the need for a right heart when receiving the sacraments (1 Cor. 11) and, it would follow that a right heart is just as important in the person who administers the sacrament or he will find himself administering judgement to himself. Is holiness the only requirement to administer the sacraments? Is it better to receive the sacraments from a holy layman than an unholy clergy-man. What happens in a home church where no one is ordained. These are not an easy issue as some would follow a belief of apostolic succession, of a priesthood which can trace its roots back through a succession of ordained men through to the apostles, while others would claim that there is no place for ordination in the church at all. Many evangelical churches permit the laity to administer the sacraments, do the laity do so in their own right or under the authority of the ordained minister.

It is difficult to give a hard and fast rule that must not be broken. When considering the problem, it is necessary to distinguish between the ordinary and the extraordinary ministry of the sacraments. On Paul's first missionary journey he travelled through Turkey and founded a number of churches and on his return journey he again visited these cities and appointed elders in the new churches Acts 14:21-23. These churches were only a few months old and men inexperienced in Christianity were thrust into the leadership role. In his advice to Timothy, I Tim 5:22, Paul advised him not to be quick to give authority to anyone. Timothy was ministering in an established but troubled church. The multitude of different circumstances that the church finds itself in will demand flexibility in whom it permits to administer the sacraments. Below is an attempt to give some guidance.

The Ordinary Ministry of the Sacraments

Ordination is a process whereby a person who is recognized by an assembly as having the call of God upon his life and the gifting for ministry and is set aside for that ministry. This involves not only the right but the obligation to minister the word, to administer the sacraments and to assist his flock in finding forgiveness of sins, Matt 16:19, John 20:20. This ministry does not come from the increased authority given to him by God to minister in his own name, to the contrary it should be a losing of self. Schmidt says of the role of the ordained minister that "... in all these functions the minister does not act in his own name, but, as by the authority, so also in the name of Christ; all the effect, therefore, that follows the Word preached proceeds not from him but from God" (1961, 605). The first and most important criterion for administering the sacrament is an acknowledgement that the person is acting instrumentally and has nothing to give of his own.

While the old order had a clear distinction between priests, who were set aside for the holy ritual of the people of Israel (Ex 28:41, 29:9, 29, 33,35; 32:29) and the laity. This is not the case in the new order. Now each man and woman is his own priest with direct access to God and fully accountable for his own soul. A second criterion for a person who administers the sacraments is a clear understanding that he does not operate as a priest with powers and rights of access to God that ordinary believers do not have.

The third criterion is that the person, whenever possible, should not be a new believer. The scripture warns about not giving authority to believers quickly. A new believer is not likely to understand what it is he is doing and the grace that is present and so is likely not to treat the sacrament with the respect that it is due. The fourth is that the person should be of sound character. The qualification set out in 1 Timothy for elders and deacons are essentially tests of character and respect in the community, not of spirituality. When a person who is regarded poorly, with cause, by the world, administers the sacraments it brings the church into disrepute in the world. They can say that Christians worship a man who was condemned as a criminal and they are led by men who are no better.

The final criterion is that the person should be one who is recognized by the assembly as one who can preach the word among them. The way the Word is present in the spoken word and in the sacraments are inseparably linked.

It should be understood that there are many layworkers that would fit into these categories.

The Extraordinary Ministry of the Sacraments

It is not uncommon that a church, particularly in the country, does not to have available the regular services of an ordained pastor or a lay worker meeting the qualifications above. At other times there may be an emergency and it is not likely that the person will live till an ordained pastor is available. Should a lay-worker, who does not meet the qualifications I have set administer the sacraments, is it valid and was the grace of the sacraments given?

The answer is "yes". The sacraments are God's gift and as the grace is given irrespective of the spiritual state of the ordained pastor, so the grace is given whether there is ordination or not. To say otherwise again suggests that the blessings are dependent on the faithfulness and worthiness of a man and not the nature of God. This is not to say that laymen should be handing out the sacraments without any regard to church order when "qualified" men are available. The firm way that Paul dealt with the disorder in the Corinthian church shows how critical order is to a church that is pleasing to God. Lutheran practice when it comes to the lay administration of the sacraments is quite sound. The sacraments should be administered by a person qualified through ordination but when circumstances dictated that a lay worker give the sacrament, he reports it to the pastor who enquires if that baptism was performed in the name of the triune God. If so it is regarded as a valid baptism and the church is told of the circumstances of its administration and told to regard it as valid (Liebeldt. Pers. Com. 1997). Thanksgiving, not reproof is the correct response.

CONCLUSION

I started this book searching for an understanding of the sacraments, uncertain in which direction that search would take. It has been a voyage of discovery. There is very little direct teaching in the New Testament about the sacraments and so much of my understanding of the sacraments came from an understanding of the whole New Testament. This included the nature of grace and Christ. No longer do I see the sacraments as empty signs offering nothing that cannot be found in other spiritual exercises. I have come to understand them as full of grace and therefore, powerful tools in the perfecting of godliness in the believer.

I have concluded that when grace is encountered in the sacraments it guards against three errors:

1. A legalistic attempt to climb to heaven as with Rome,
2. A spiritual interpretation of religion which is reduced to inward experience as with Zwingli; and,
3. The reduction of Christianity to a set of theological beliefs without an inner life.

I hope this is your conclusion also.

GLOSSARY

Anabaptist	A term meaning re-baptists, a name they objected to as it implied that the first baptism was valid.
Ex Opere Operato	This Latin phrase can be translated "the work that has been worked" Expiation The forgiveness of a person's sin as an entity in itself. It is not the word used to describe the reconciliation of an angry god with a person.
Impetration	Pleading for favour form a profound sense of need
Mystery Religions	These were a group of oriental religions that had wider acceptance in the Roman Empire than the official cults. They required secret initiation and offered personal involvement, emotional stimulation and life after death. Persian Mithraism was the main rival to

	Christianity during the second and third centuries and had many common practices and terminologies.(Bromiley, 1988, Vol 4, 113-4)
Paedobaptism	The practice of baptising infants
Simony	Distribuiting the blessings of Christianity for financial benefit (Acts 8: 9-25).
Transubstantiation	A term first used by Hildebert of Tours in the early 13th century and which soon took on common usage. It was an attempt to describe philosophically the reality of Christ's presence the Catholic associated with the Mass. The philosophical arguments associated with this doctrine were developed with such philosophical sophistication that they would remain plausible to Catholic scholars for centuries. It stated that the bread and wine became the physically present body and blood
Ubiquity	The doctrine states that Christ's resurrection body is located only in heaven

WORKS CITED

Adamthwaite, Murray. The Miqveh in Intertestamental Judaism *Buried History* Volume 28 Number 2 June 1992.

Althaus, Paul. *The Theology of Martin Luther.* (Fortress Press: Philadelphia. 1966).

Salvation Army, International Headquarters *The Salvation Army - Handbook of Doctrine.* (The Salvation Army: London, 1969).

Atkinson, James. *Martin Luther and the Birth of Protestantism,* (Penguin: Harmondsworth, 1968).

Baillie, Donald M.U.D. *The Theology of the Sacraments.* (Faber and Faber: London, U.D.)

Bainton, Roland. *The Reformation of the Sixteenth Century.* (Hodder and Stoughton: London, 1969).

Bainton, Roland. *Here I Stand, A life of Martin Luther* (Festival Books: Nashville 1978).

Beasley-Murray, Paul. *Radical Believers.* (Baptist Union of Great Britain: 1992).

Berkouwer, G.C. *The Sacrament.* (Eerdmans: Grand Rapids. 1969).

Braaten, Carl E. *Principles of Lutheran Theology.* (Fortune Press: Philadelphia, 1983).

Calvin, John. *Calvin's Institutes.* (Associated Publishers and Authors Inc.: Grand Rapids, U.D).

Edersheim, Alfred. *The Life and Times of Jesus the Messiah.* (Eerdmans Printing Co: Grand Rapids, 1977).

Gabler, Ulrich. *Huldrych Zwingli, His Life and Work.* (T&T Clark Limited: Edinbrough, 1987).

Hamann, Henry P. *On Being a Christian.* (Lutheran Publishing Co.: Adelaide, 1989).

Hoad, Jack. *The Baptist.* (Grace Publication: London, 1986).

Hughes, Philip J. *The Pentecostals in Australia.* (Australian Government Publishing Service: Canberra,1996).

Kittel, G. Ed. *Theological Dictionary of the New Testament A-N.* (Eerdmans Publishing Company: Grand Rapids,. 1967).

Matros, Joseph. *Doors to the Sacred.* (SCM: London. 1981).

Montgomery, John W. *Damned Through the Church.* (Bethany Fellowship Inc.: Minneapolis, 1970).

Murray, John. *Christian Baptism.* (Presbyterian and Reformed Publishing Co: Phillipsburg, 1980).

Packer, G.H.W. *The Morning Star.* (W.B. Eerdmans Publishing Co: Grand Rapids, 1965).

Plass, Ewald M. *What Luther Says - An Anthology.* (Concordia Publishing House: St. Louis. 1972).

Renfrey, Lionel E.W Anglican-Lutheran Discussions in Australia. *Lutheran Theological Journal.* (Lutheran Church of Australia: Adelaide, 1976).

Rilliet, Jean. *Zwingli The Third Man of the Reformation.* (Lutterworth: London, 1964).

Ryle, J.C. *Five English Reformers.* (Banner of Truth: Edinburgh, 1981).

Schlink, Edmond. *The Doctrine of Baptism.* (Concordia: St Louis, 1972).

Schwarz, Hans. *Divine Communication.* (Fortress Press: Philadelphia, 1985).

Sasse, Herman. *We Confess, The sacraments* (CPH: Saint Louis, 1985).

Stevenson, J. *A New Eusebius.* (SPCK: Londo,. 1970).

Schmidt, Herman, *Doctrinal Theology of the Evangelical Lutheran Church.* Reprint (Augsburg Publishing House: Minneapolis 1961).

Tappert, Theodore G. *The Book of Concord.* (Fortress Press: Philadelphia, 1956).

Thomas, W.H. Griffith. *The Principles of Theology.* (Church Book Room Press: London, 1963).

Wagner, Mervyn. Luther's Baptismal Theology, *Lutheran Theological Journal,* (Openbook Publishers Adelaide Vol. 31, No. 2 1997).

Watson, Philip S., *Let God be God.* (Fortress Press: Philadelphia, 1966).

INTERNET SITES

Augustine — *De Symbolo ad Catechumenos* [online] URL http://ccel.wheaton.edu/fathers/NPNF1-03/on the creed.html [accessed 22 December 1997].

Booth Bramwell — *On the Sacraments* New Frontier Vol 14, Num 12 [online] URL http://205.184.30.5/sal-army/new frontier/1412/1212.htm) [accessed 7 July 1997].

Council of Trent — *Decree Concerning Justification* Sixth Session [online] URL http://www.ismsa.edu./~history/trent6.html [accessed 17 August 1997].

-------- *Decree Concerning Original Sin* Fifth Session [online] URL http://www.ismsa.edu./~history/trent5.html [accessed 17 August 1997].

-------- *Decree Concerning the Sacraments* Seventh Session [online] URL http://www.ismsa.edu./~history/trent7.html [accessed 17 August 1997].

-------- *Doctrine on the Sacrifice of the Mass* Twenty-second Session [online] URL http://history.hanover.edu/early/trent/ct22cmas.htm [accessed 17 August 1997].

Cyril of Jerusalem *Lecture 23. On the Mysteries* [online] URL http://ccel.wheaton.edu/fathers/NPNF2-07/Cyril/Lectures/t1.htm#t1.htm.24 [accessed 27 September 1997].

Fanning William H.W Baptism *Catholic Encyclopedia* [online] URL http://www.knight.org/advent/cathen/02258b.htm [accessed 10 August 1997].

Fieser James Peter Lombard *The Internet encyclopedia of Philosophy* [online] URL http://www.utm.edu/research/iep/l/lombard.htm [accessed 16 July 1997].

Fieser James Thomas Aquinas *The Internet Encyclopedia of Philosophy* [online] URL http://www.utm.edu/research/iep/a/aquinas.htm [assessed 16 July 1997].

Frontinus, Sextus Julius *Stratagems* [online] URL http://penelope.uchicago.edu/Thayer/E/Roman/Texts/Frontinus/Strategemata/4*.html

Irenaeus *Against Heresies Book 2* [online] URL http://ccel.wheaton.edu/fathers/anf-01/iren/iren2.html#section2 [accessed 29 September 1997].

Justin Martyr *The First Apology of Justin* [online] URL http://ccel.wheaton.edu/fathers/

ANF-01/just/justap1index.html [accessed 29 September 1997].

Kennedy D.J.   Sacraments *Catholic Encyclopaedia* [online] URL http://www.csn.net/advent/cathen/13295a.ht m#IV [accessed 22 July 1997].

Pohle J.   Sacrifice of the Mass *Catholic Encyclopedia* [online]   URL http://www.knight,org/advent/cathen/10006a .htm [accessed 2october 1997]

Quaker Home Services. *Quaker Views* [online] URL http://www.quaker.org/BYM/qviews1.html [accessed 12 July 1997].

Tertullian   *On Proscriptions Against Heretics*_[online] URL   http://ccel.wheaton.edu/fathers/ ANF-03/tertullian/part2/prescription_against _heretics.html [accessed 29 September 1997]

www.ingramcontent.com/pod-product-compliance
Lightning Source LLC
Chambersburg PA
CBHW050553280326
41933CB00011B/1831